© 1990 Franklin Watts

Franklin Watts Inc.
387 Park Avenue South
New York, NY 10016

Editor: Hazel Poole
Design: K and Co
Consultant: Michael Chinery

Printed in Italy

Library of Congress Cataloging-in-Publication Data

Watts, Barrie.
    Ladybugs / Barrie Watts.
        p.   cm. — (Keeping minibeasts)
    Summary: Discusses the feeding and reproductive habits of ladybugs
and suggests ways to raise and breed them domestically.
    ISBN 0-531-14043-1
    1. Ladybirds as pets — Juvenile literature. 2. Ladybirds — Juvenile
literature. [1. Ladybugs. 2. Ladybugs — Collection and
preservation.] I. Title. II. Series.
SF459.L33W37   1990
638'.638'.5796 — dc20   89-49716
                                                                 CIP
                                                                 AC

Each kind of ladybug has its own pattern with up to 24 spots. They all like to eat aphids and other small insect pests and are a great help to gardeners and farmers around the world.

Each different kind of ladybug likes to eat a particular kind of aphid or other insect, which means that each species of ladybug has its preferred habitat. They will mate and lay their eggs near to the aphids.

Gardens are excellent places to find ladybugs. Coniferous forests can be good for certain kinds, but some ladybugs, like the two spot, can be found everywhere.

Collecting ladybugs

Ladybugs are small insects so you will need only small plastic containers and a paintbrush to collect them. A warm sunny day in spring or summer is the best time to look for them.

Ladybugs move very quickly, so when you collect them, make sure that the lid of your container has airholes and is on tight. Put a leaf inside for them to cling to.

The best way to collect a ladybug is to either use a paintbrush to guide it into your box, or just let it walk onto your hand.

Never pick them up with your fingers as they can easily be damaged. When they are disturbed, ladybugs normally withdraw their legs and cling to whatever they are on. Wait until they start moving again, then you can guide them into the container.

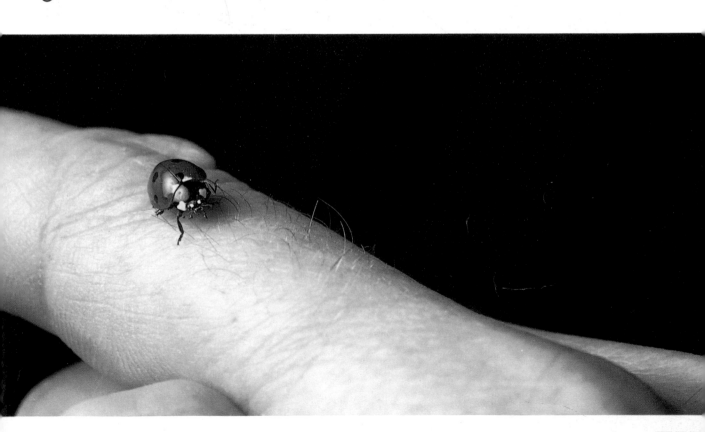

Housing

Ladybugs can easily be kept in a large clear plastic box or an aquarium with a piece of an old sheet or similar material stretched over the top. Provide some leaves and twigs for them to crawl over and to shelter under.

Spray a little water inside regularly because they need moisture just like other insects. Ladybugs also need warmth so keep them on a light and airy window sill. If not, they will hide and you will not see them.

Make a net cage

If you would like to breed ladybugs, the best place to do this is outside in the backyard during the spring.

You can make a net cage or buy one. Find a plant with plenty of aphids on it.

Place several ladybugs on the plant and enclose it in the cage to keep them from escaping. If the cage is in a sunny position, the ladybugs will mate and lay eggs. You can study the eggs as they develop.

Useful ladybugs

When ladybugs are active, they are always looking for food. They like to feed on aphids such as greenfly which can be found on roses and blackfly which can be found on beans.

A ladybug can eat up to thirty aphids each day and the larva (young ladybug) can eat as many as fifty. To enable the ladybugs to breed in your cage you must give them plenty to eat.

You can collect aphids from gardens and hedges. Cut the stems of plants that are infested with aphids and place the stems in a jar of water. This will keep the plant fresh for some time so the aphids can feed on it. The aphids will breed very quickly. Each one may have several babies in a day.

Put the jar of cut food in your cage or tank. You can also brush some aphids into the cage or tank each day. Make sure that the ladybugs get a regular supply of fresh food.

Life-cycle

Ladybugs mate when the sun has warmed them and they are active. The female will lay her eggs on the underside of leaves near a supply of aphids because the tiny larvae will eat these when they hatch.

Sometimes the larvae will eat each other if there are no aphids nearby. As they get bigger, the larvae will eat continually, searching for aphids to eat throughout the day and night.

Fully-grown larvae measure about 15mm (½ inch) long. After they have stopped feeding, they will glue themselves to the plant on which they have been hunting.

After two hours, a ladybug larva sheds its skin and turns into a pupa. A few hours later, the outside of the pupa is dry and well-camouflaged.

The adult ladybug emerges from the pupa after five days and will spend the rest of the summer feeding. It will then go to sleep for the winter.

Releasing your ladybugs

Since ladybugs eat garden pests, it is a good idea to release them in your garden or backyard. Then you would not need to use chemical sprays to get rid of any aphids that are harming your plants.

Unusual facts

Young ladybug larvae inject saliva into their prey and suck out the contents. Older larvae are able to chew up the whole aphid.

Adult ladybugs get their spots as they dry out after emerging from the pupae.

There are about four thousand different kinds of ladybug living around the world.

Most ladybugs are carnivorous, that is they eat other animals. The yellow and black 22-spot ladybug is a vegetarian, and eats various plants.

Ladybugs can bite and will give a sharp nip if roughly handled.

Index

JUN   2008   WI